Delusionism

Volume 01

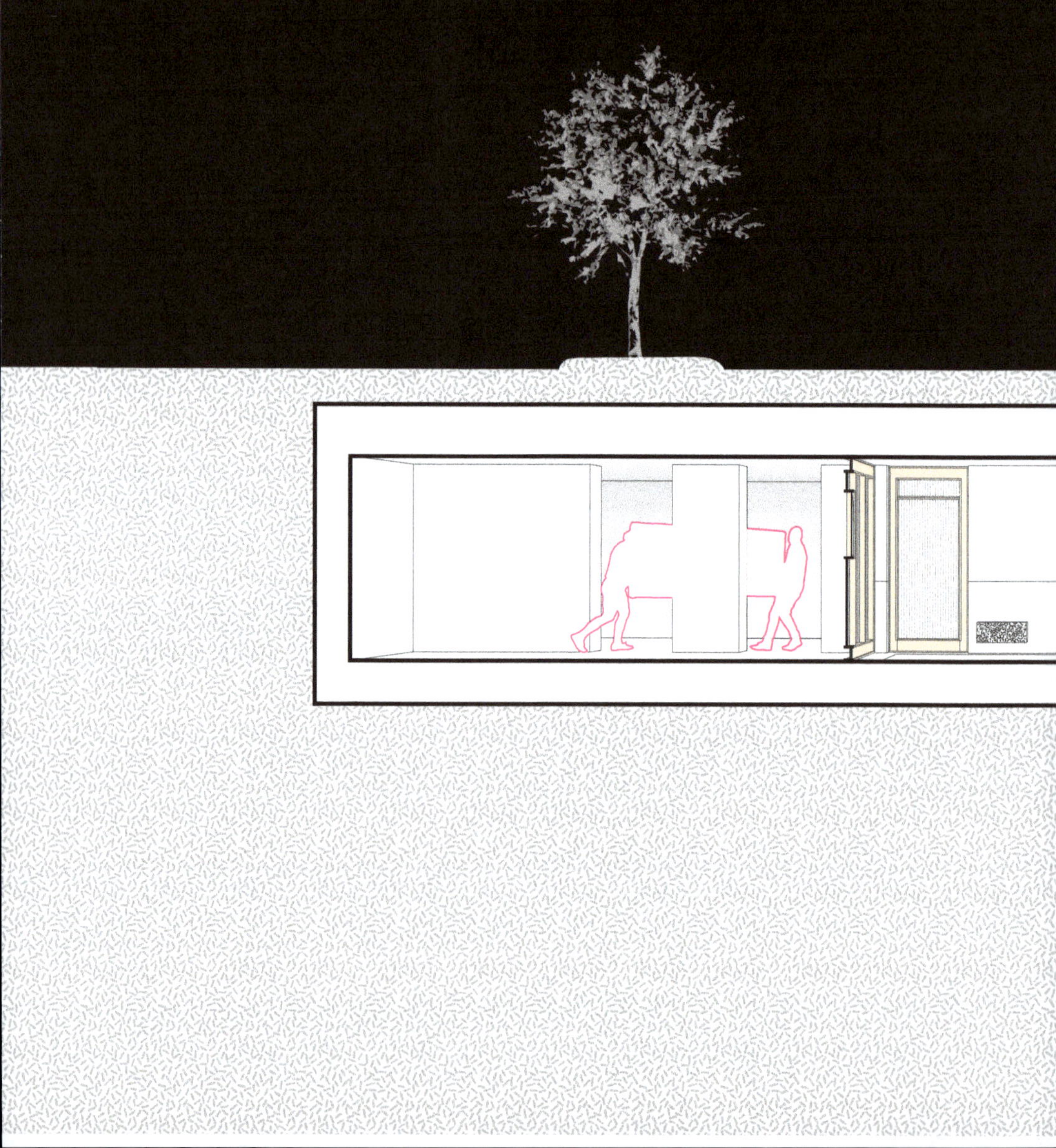

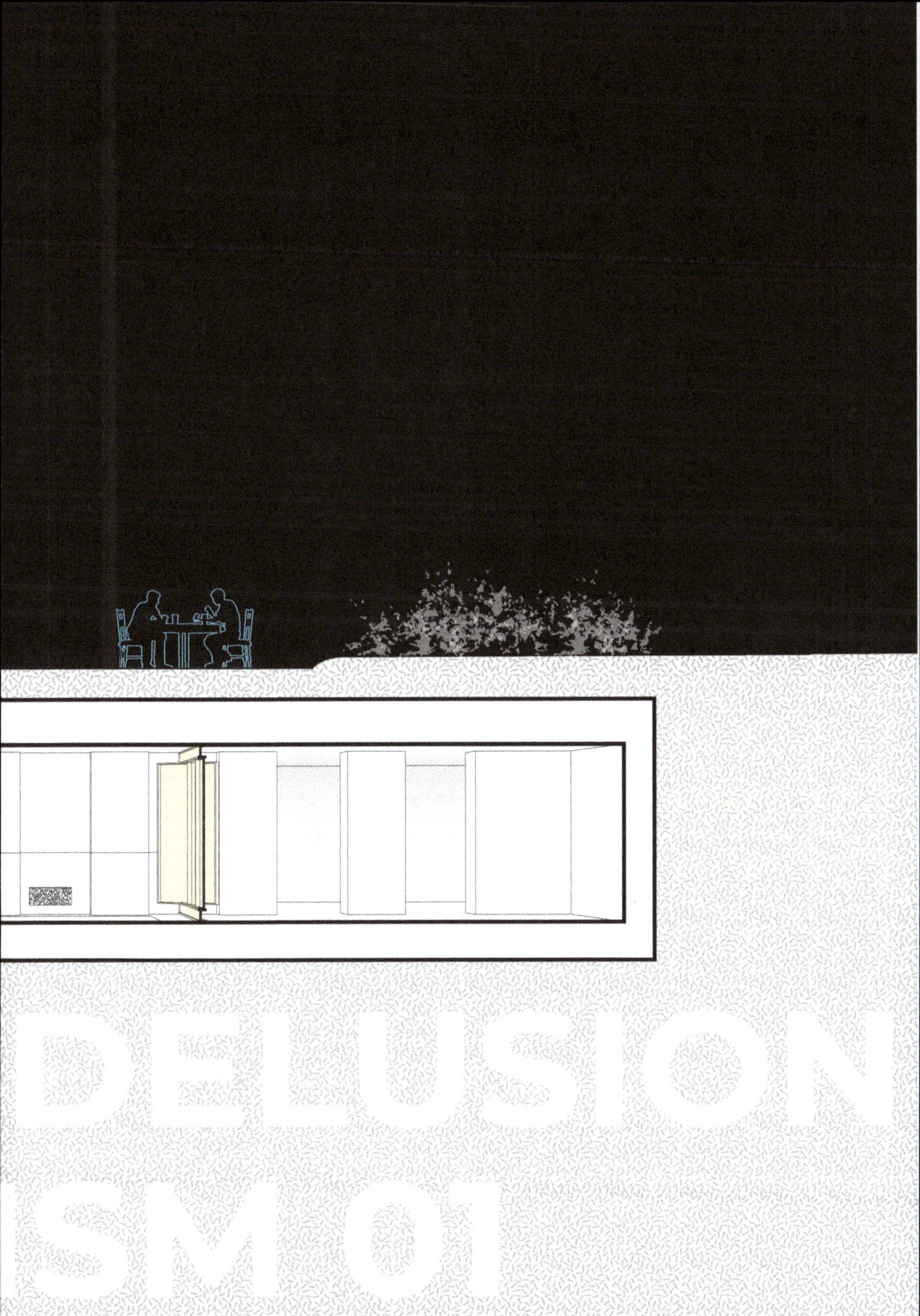

DELUSION
ISM 01

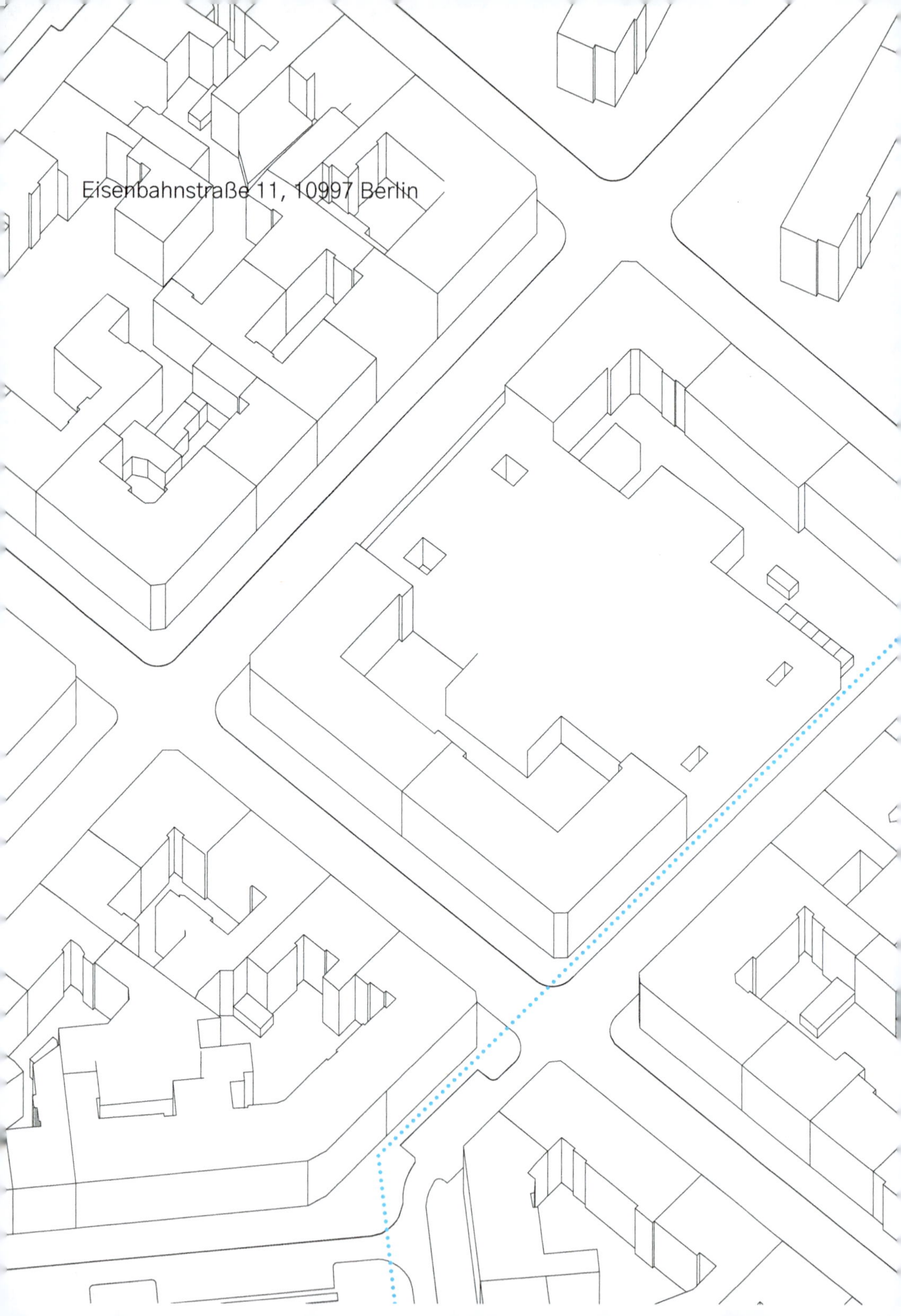
Eisenbahnstraße 11, 10997 Berlin

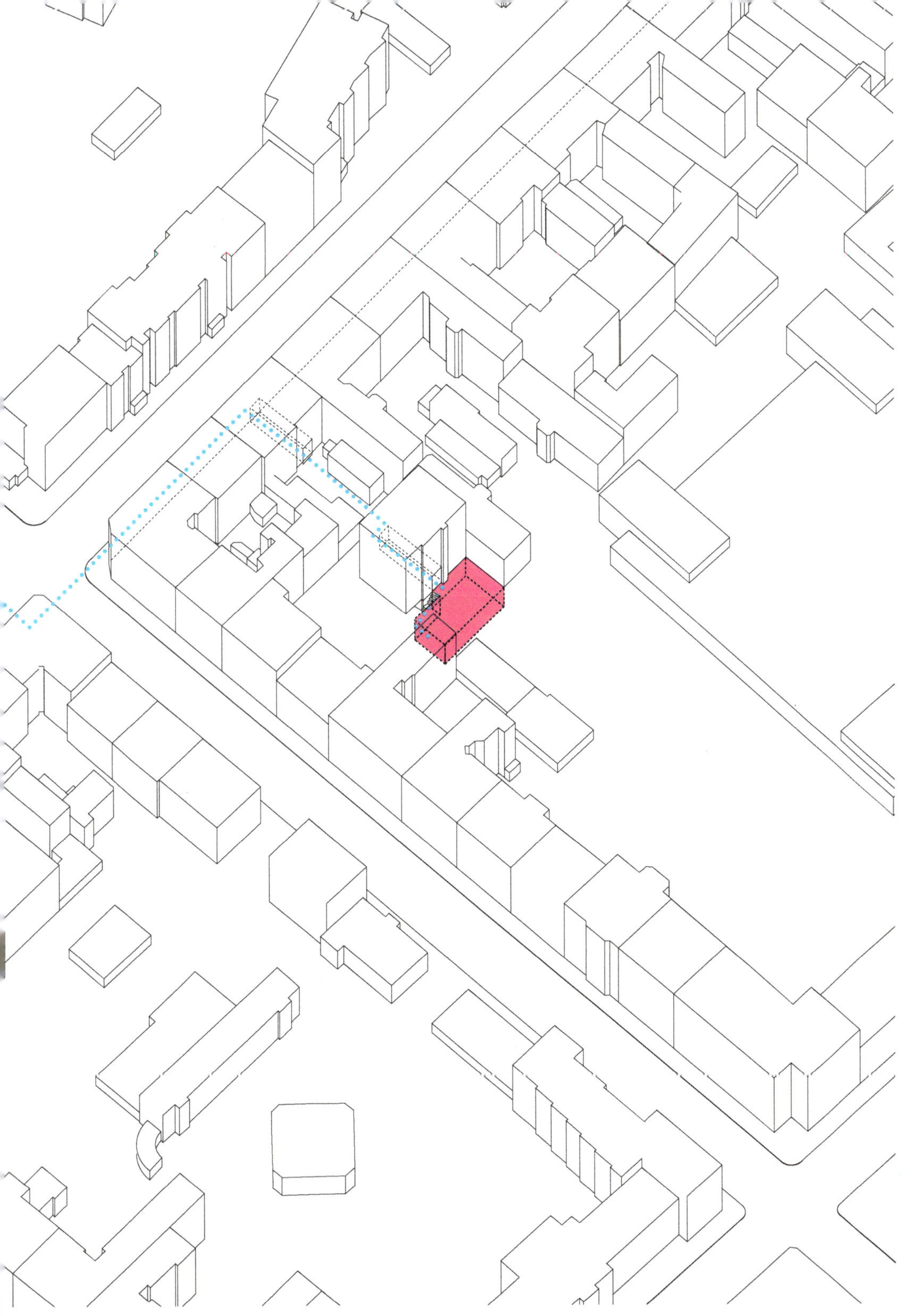

intro

A minimum definition of Delusionist action
Volume 01

No. 1 We trust intuition and human nature before tradition or normality
by any means necessary.

No. 2 Intuition is not a feeling. Intuition is the response to a topical
understanding of the time.

No. 3 Nothing is permanent, therefore answers are never timeless.

No. 4 Art is interpretation, replication, a regurgitation of one's current
reality; a reaction.

No. 5 Now we move past the spectacle of art in order to restore art as
the spectacle for thought.

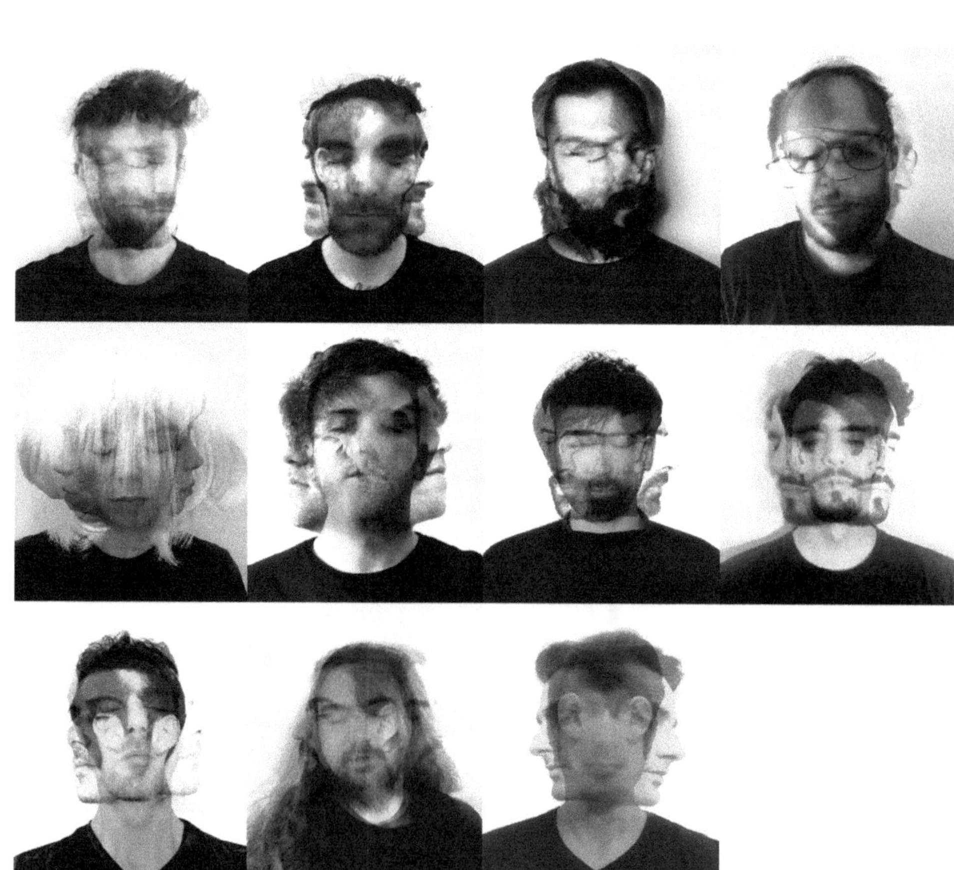

Compiled by
Kevin Driscoll
Rion Philbin

Designed by
So & So Studio

With help from
Alessandro Barbieri
Andrei Dan Mușetescu
Apo Kardamov
Attilio Delucchi Baroni
Francesca Maculan
Iulian Ivan
Nikola Milanovic
Patrick Haggerty
Vlad Zangor

No. 1 We trust intuition and human nature before tradition or normality
by any means necessary.

Aesthetics: THE BEAUTIFUL IS not ALWAYS TRUE AND GOOD
So & So Studio

Make an image of our aesthetics with their intoxication and their desire to intoxicate. Now see human beings as they are in their current state; isolated and unable to connect emotionally with each other and the space in which they occupy. Now consider one of these human beings confined to the cave of their own personal experience. Tell them of an architecture that relates us to our own being as it reveals feeling through layers of process, emotion, time and space. Tell them that architecture can become an experience beyond a visual gaze in which we experience both the spaces and ourselves as emotional recipients. It is to no surprise; the prisoner will not believe something can evoke such emotion from within them. It is true to them, that architecture is but an image. And it is to no surprise, they do not see the spaces that lay beyond the image, for the oversaturation has distorted their sense of depth.

In this age where materialism reigns, society is completely captivated by their desire to consume goods – enslaved by the depthless appearance of two-dimensional imagery. An obsession where there is no feeling, no reveal, no experience; everything is reduced to the surface for the purpose of seductive persuasion. It is in the hands of today's creators and their architecture to stray from this tendency to rely on shallow exterior aesthetic, void of substance. As a reaction to the over saturated ephemeral imagery, one must imagine looking beyond architecture to a new system of discovery, inhabitance, and play. Where a new vocabulary is introduced with new concepts, and an entirely new approach. There is a technological blanket of passivity that weighs the shoulders of today and prevents any and all exploration and experimentation. Thus, we are left with no surprises, no activation, lost opportunity, and no fun.

--

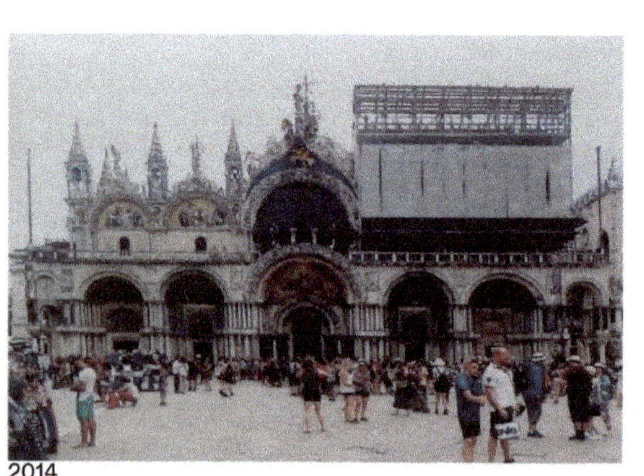

2014

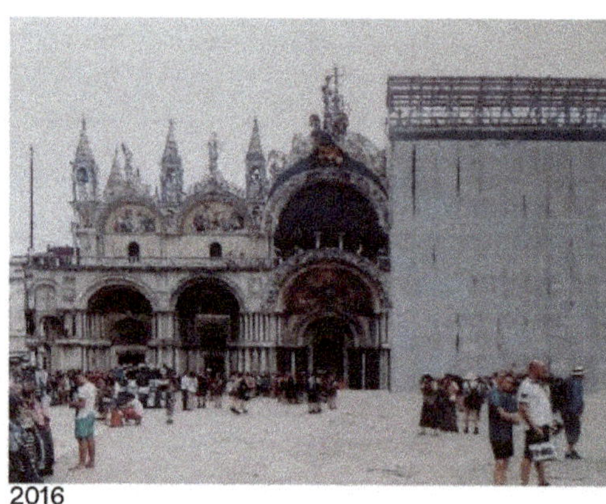

2016

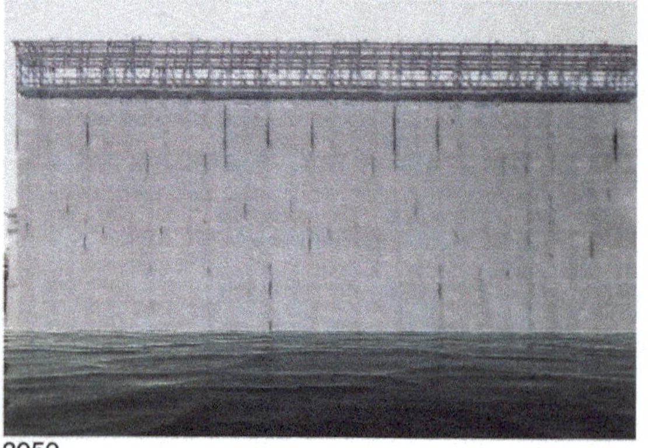

2050

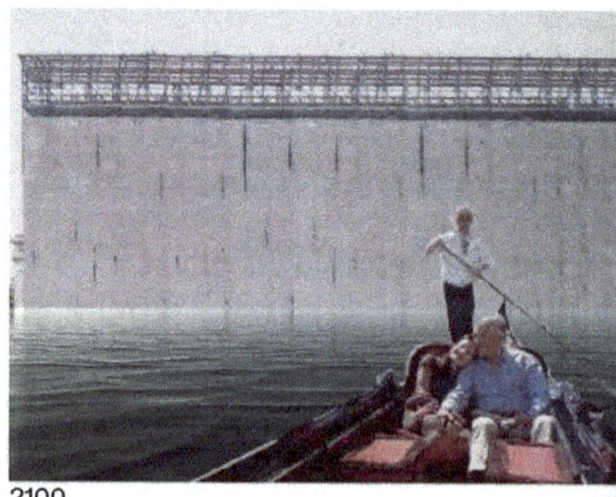

2100

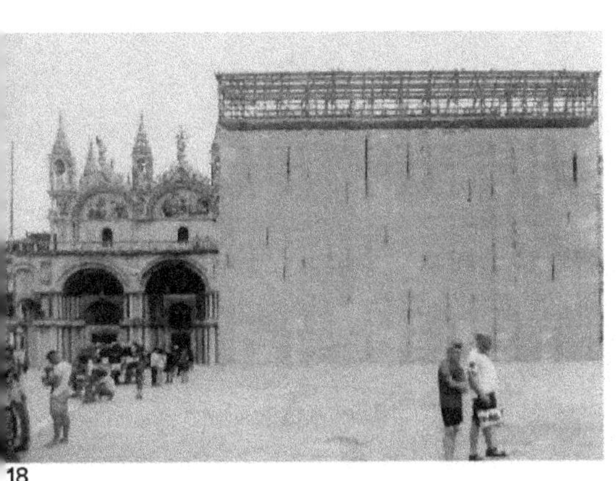

18

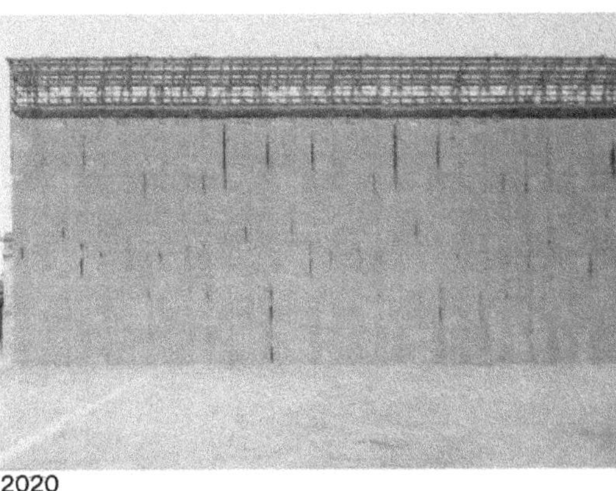

2020

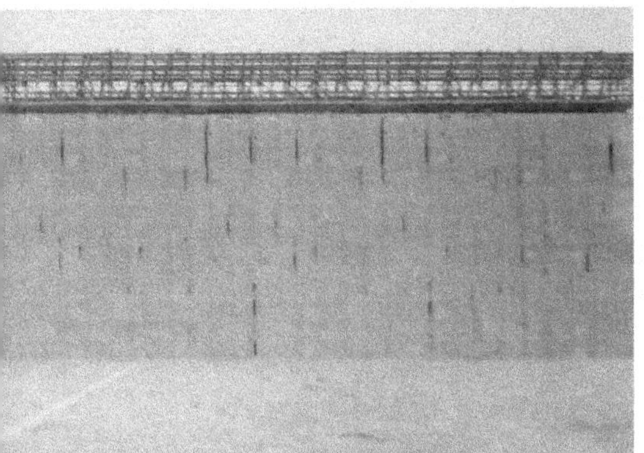

50

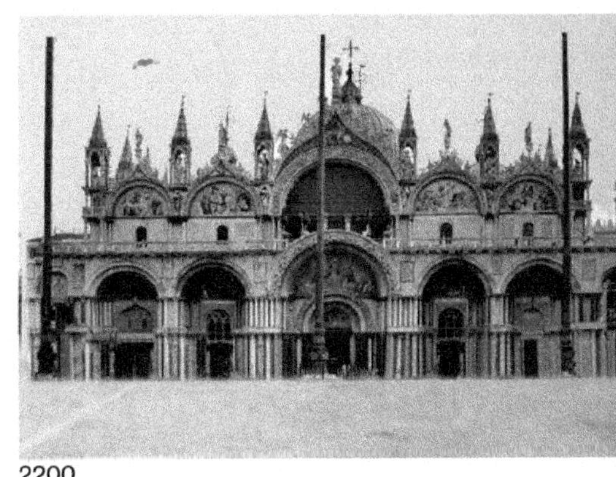

2200

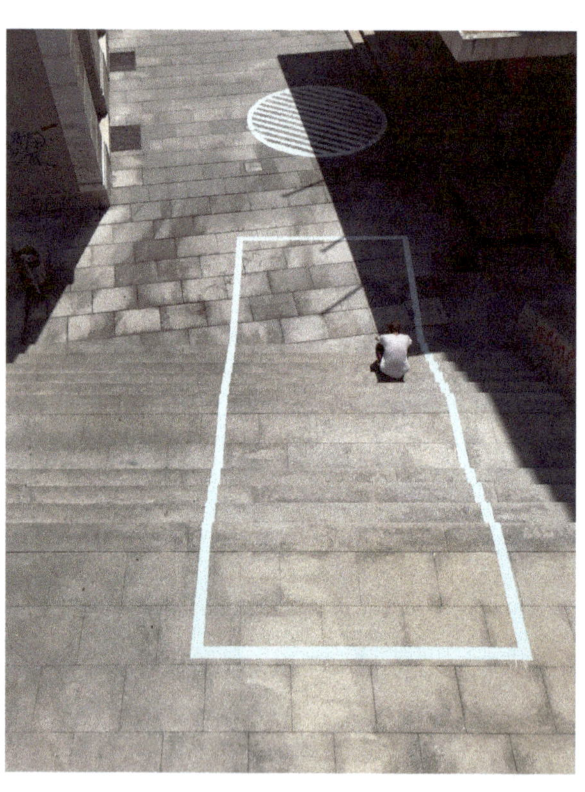

--

People do not realize the space in which they occupy and even more concerning, the space that exists beyond their gaze. I wonder what the masses are thinking about? What are they feeling? As one moves through a space, does it feel significant? Is there a context, or historical thought?

When our landmarks are garmented with scaffolding, under construction, does it change the way we see, feel or inhabit the space?

Does one even notice the garment? The photos don't stop, the tours don't stagger, we still take pictures, we still tell our friends, we still show up! We even buy postcards of something we've already experienced ourselves – but maybe the photos are more beautiful – though photoshopped.

Or maybe we need to prove to others we've been here, with a note about how lovely it is. But how do we know if we haven't truly experienced its essence?

If we garment all the monuments, the palaces and the rest of the trendy, instagrammed historical architecture and urbanity, no one would realize, no one would care. Garment them all to kill the capital image as it has killed the architectural grandiose.

Bring the space back to zero, strip it of all its meaning, only to one day allow its original character to return. to live free again. – reclaim your city.

Dear Visitors,

Due to overcrowding, forgotten significance and uninformed, uninterested guests, this site is „under construction".

Yours truly,
The few who care

--

Garment buildings and their spaces until further notice. Virtual tours of said spaces will be „temporarily" available at an off-site location that actually doesn't matter, for the experience will be consumed in the same hollow manner. Eventually, the physical form of these spaces will become irrelevant. More importantly, people will forget where they are and that they even exist. Only then, long after people have been completely consumed by this technological wormhole, will these monuments, these buildings, and these spaces, truly reveal themselves, reclaiming themselves in their entirety. Reclaimed and reborn. Now, completely forgotten, totally silent and finally alone, they will be as powerful and as imposing as ever, regaining a significance past the superficial glances. unexperienced.

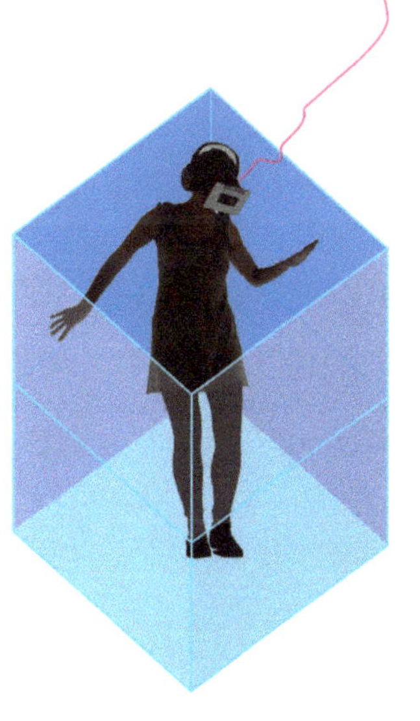
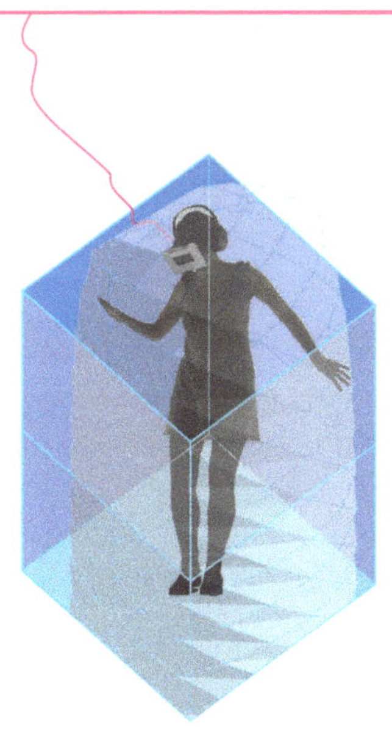

No. 2   Intuition is not a feeling. Intuition is the response to a topical
understanding of the time.

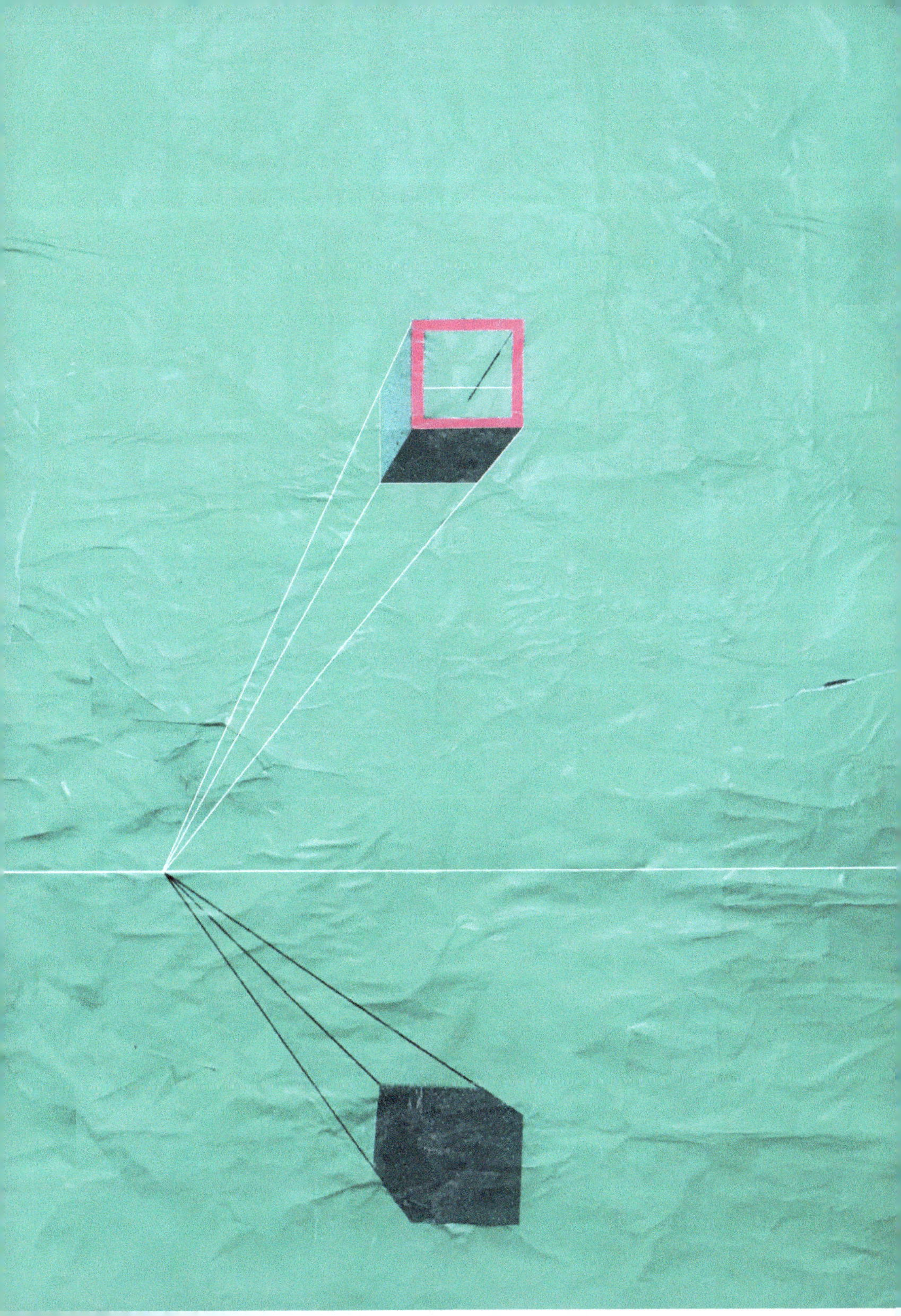

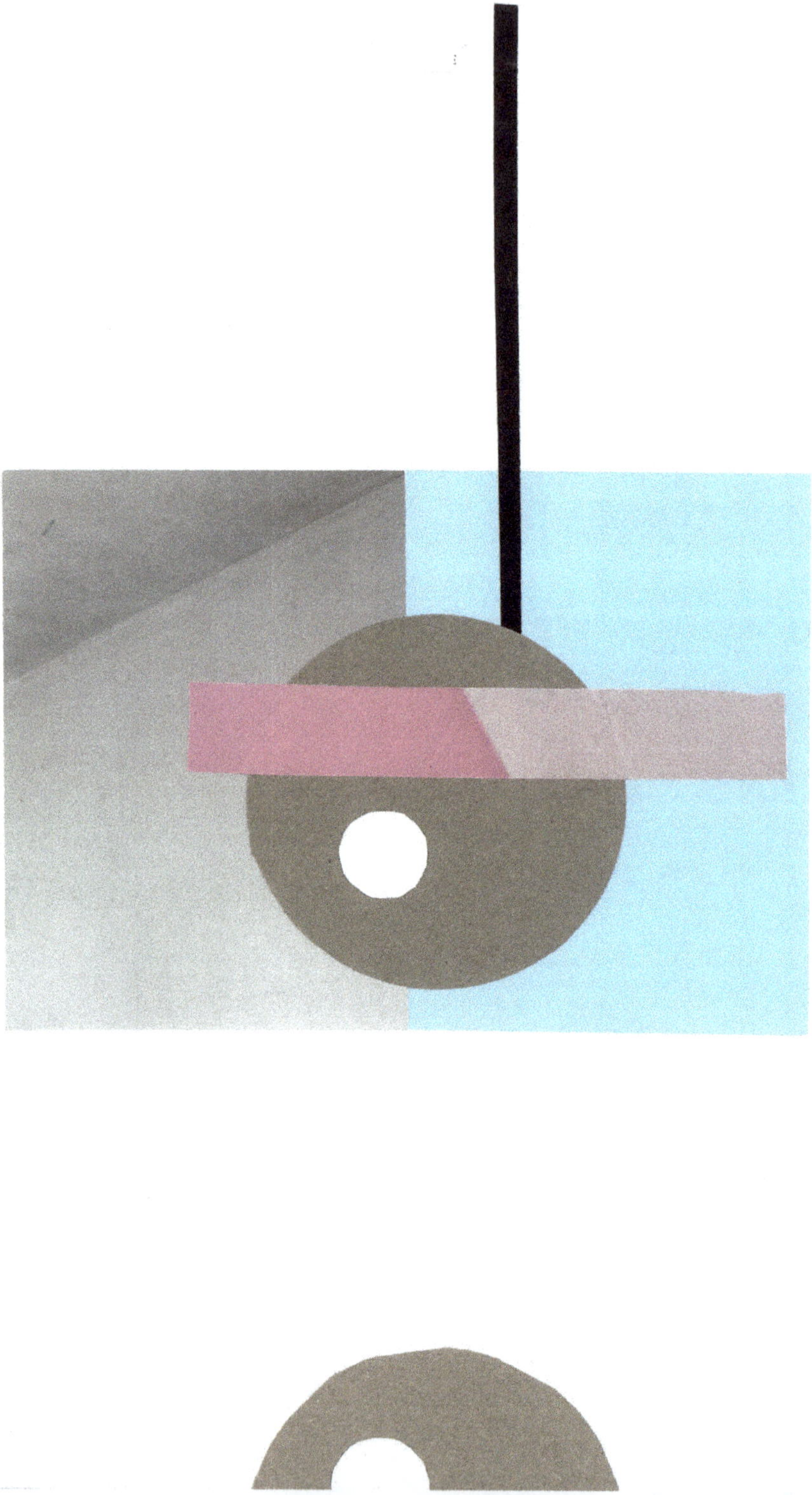

Ripped-off
So & So Studio

Jorge Luis Borges, in 1985, claims: "Space, according to the idealists, does not exist in and of itself: it is a mental phenomenon, like pain, fear, and vision, and being part of consciousness, it may in no way be said that consciousness is situated in space."

The collage began as an exercise to explore and excavate intuitive potential within each project. Form and space reduced to an essence by using residual materials: first found in magazines and later ripped off the streets of Berlin, Germany.

The challenge was depth.

Within the recording of time, space, as it is recognized in consciousness, is the artifact and evidence of moments which exist in the present. As architects, it is our responsibility to realize space in every facet of the word.

Through collage, the instantaneous results of perceived space are utilized. It is within this result where the consciousness of space becomes the viewer's perceived time. Posters from the past are taken from the streets to feed an intuitive spatial creation and understanding of the architectural future. The viewer will experience a current reality, that is a present state of a layered past. A past that was once advertising for the future, but now draws the viewer into a new spatial dimension of a hopeful future.

There was a question of copyright.

More specifically, the concept of integrity of intellectual property that exists within the IP of physical imagery vs. digital. For example, in comparing the appropriation of paper posters glued to the walls of the streets vs. google images. This inspires intrigue of value in imagery, especially in the lens of the consumer of such imagery. For the digital consumer of images, everything is fast and in your face.

The street poster format quietly (to a numb passerby) approaches you at your leisure while familiarizing you with prescribed pallets of favored CMYK combinations and thoughtful slogans, the digital RGB images act more or less as environmental tones of light designed to target dopamine in your brain as quickly as possible.

Ripped Off was born into the physical world of appropriation of common imagery in a heroic attempt to regurgitate colors and textures of the moment into timeless impressions of future space.

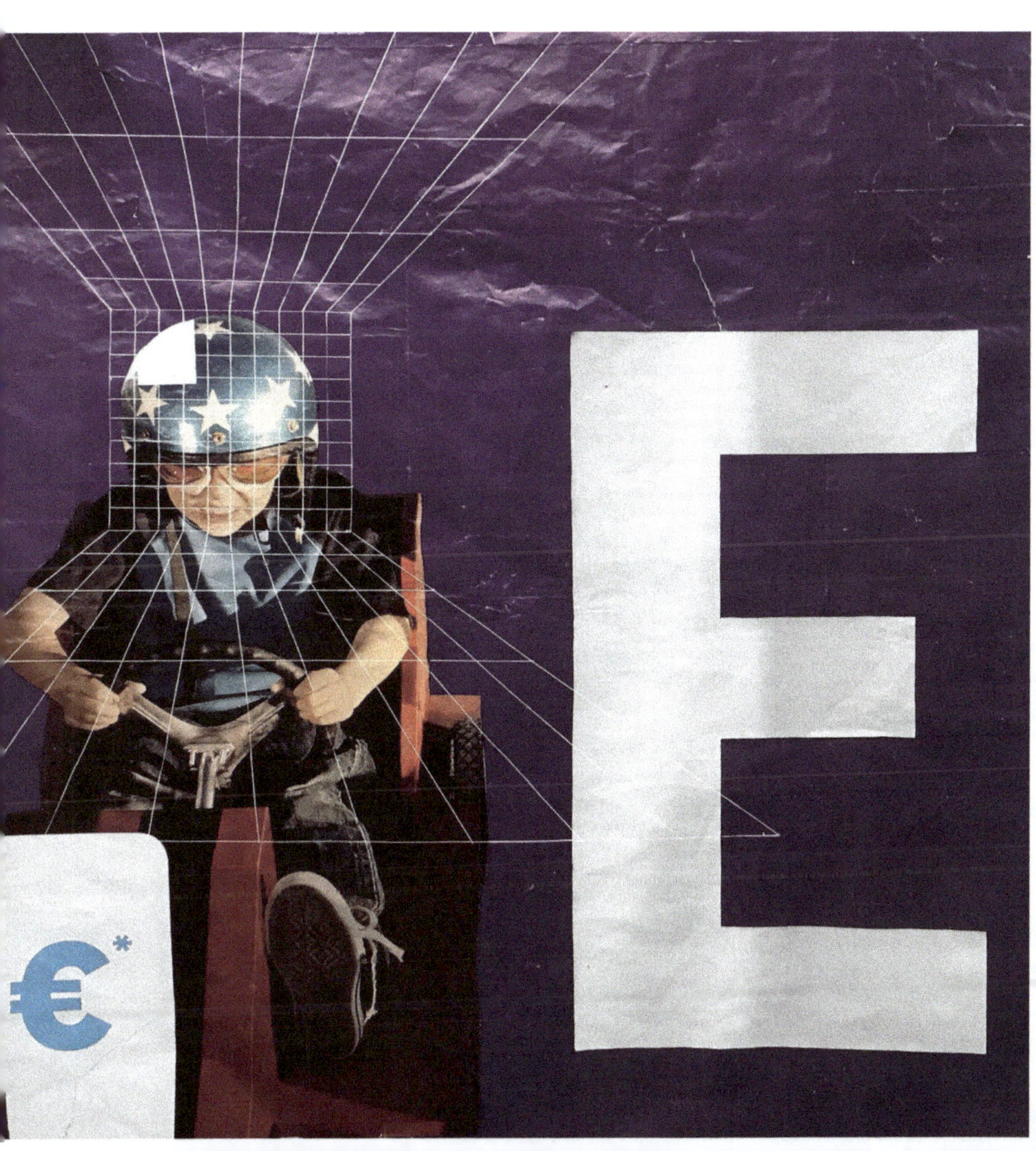

E
€*

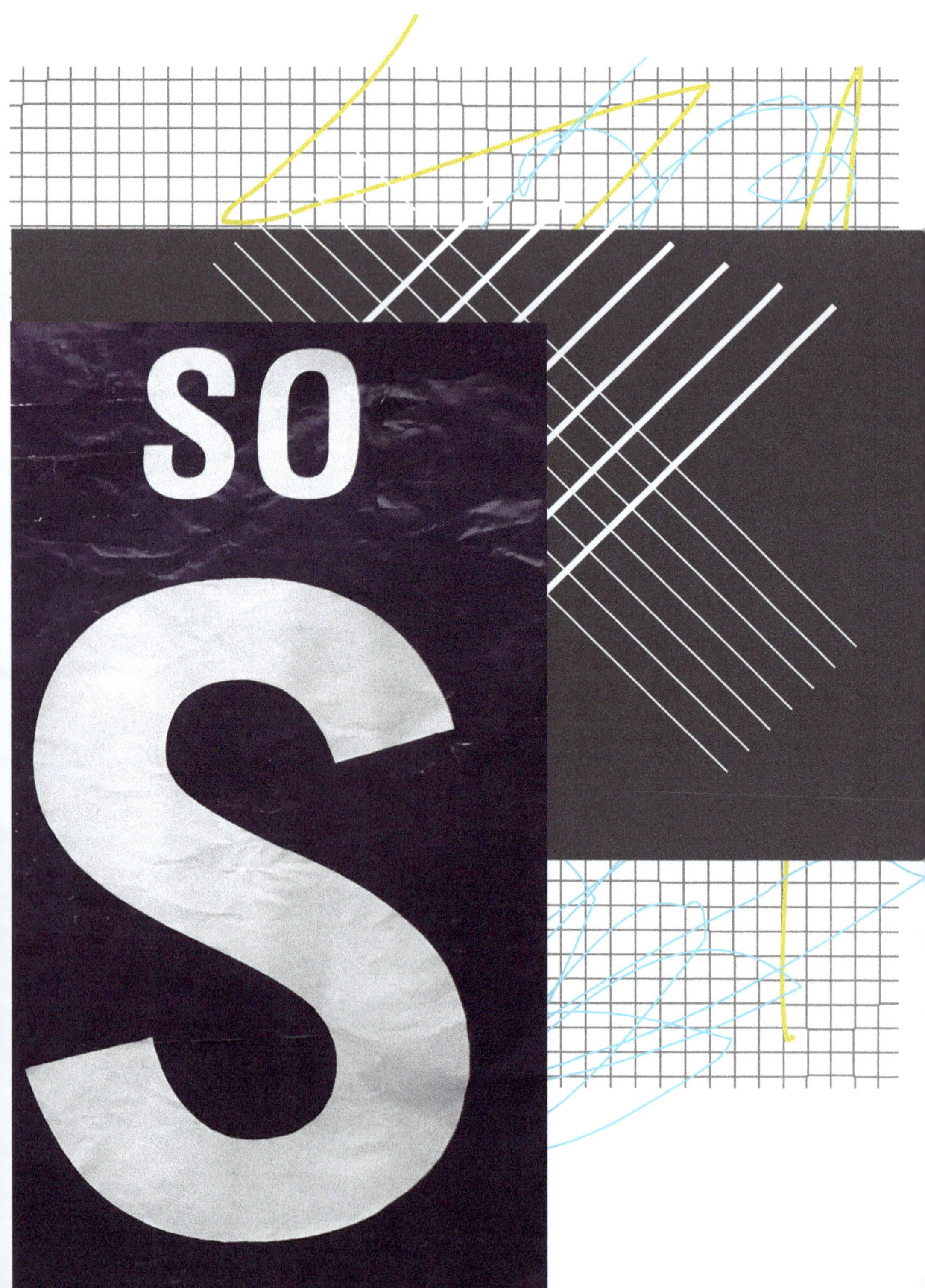
SO
S

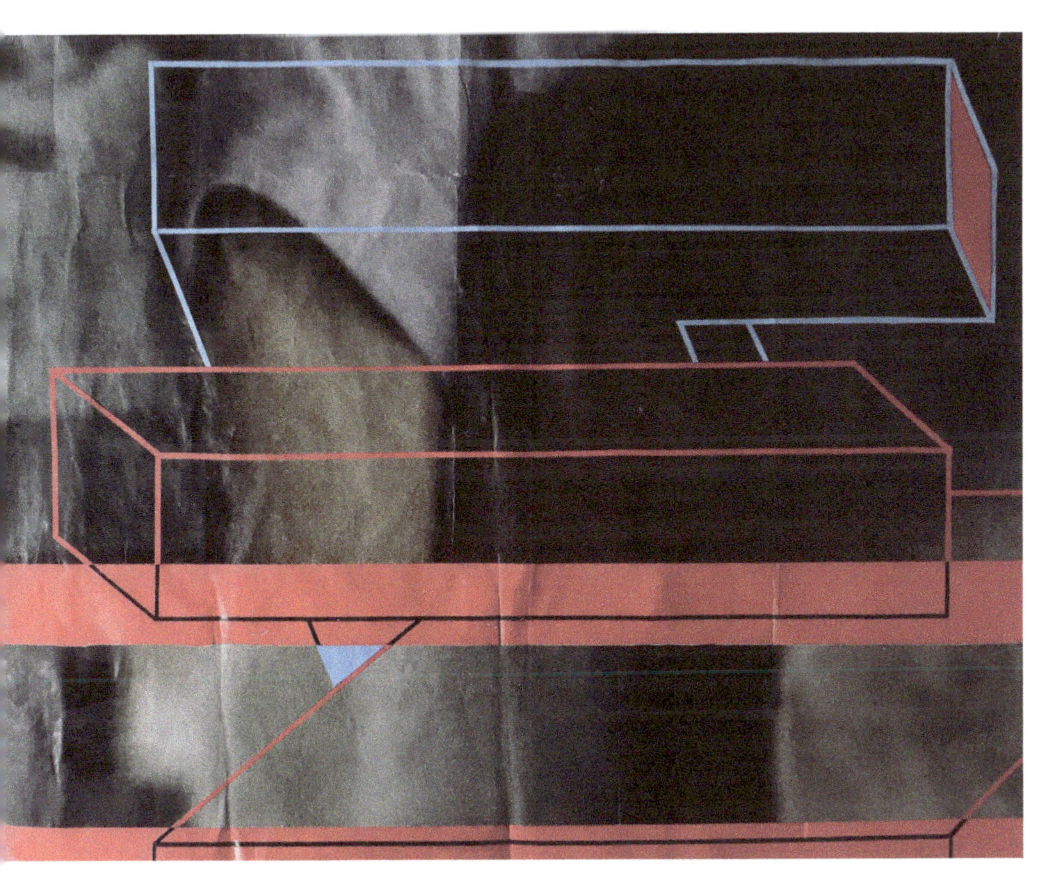

So & So Studio
Axon 2019
Collage on paper, 114 x 92cm

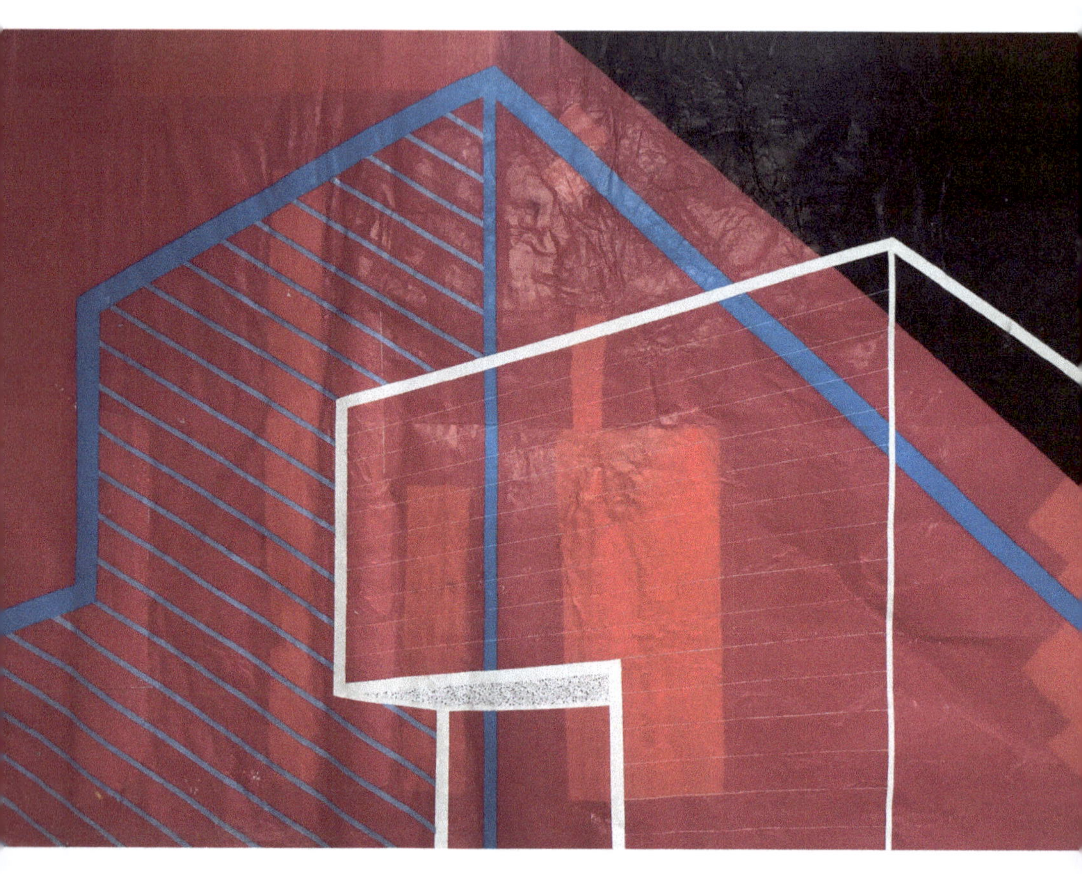

So & So Studio
unfinished 2019
Collage on paper, 250 x 175cm

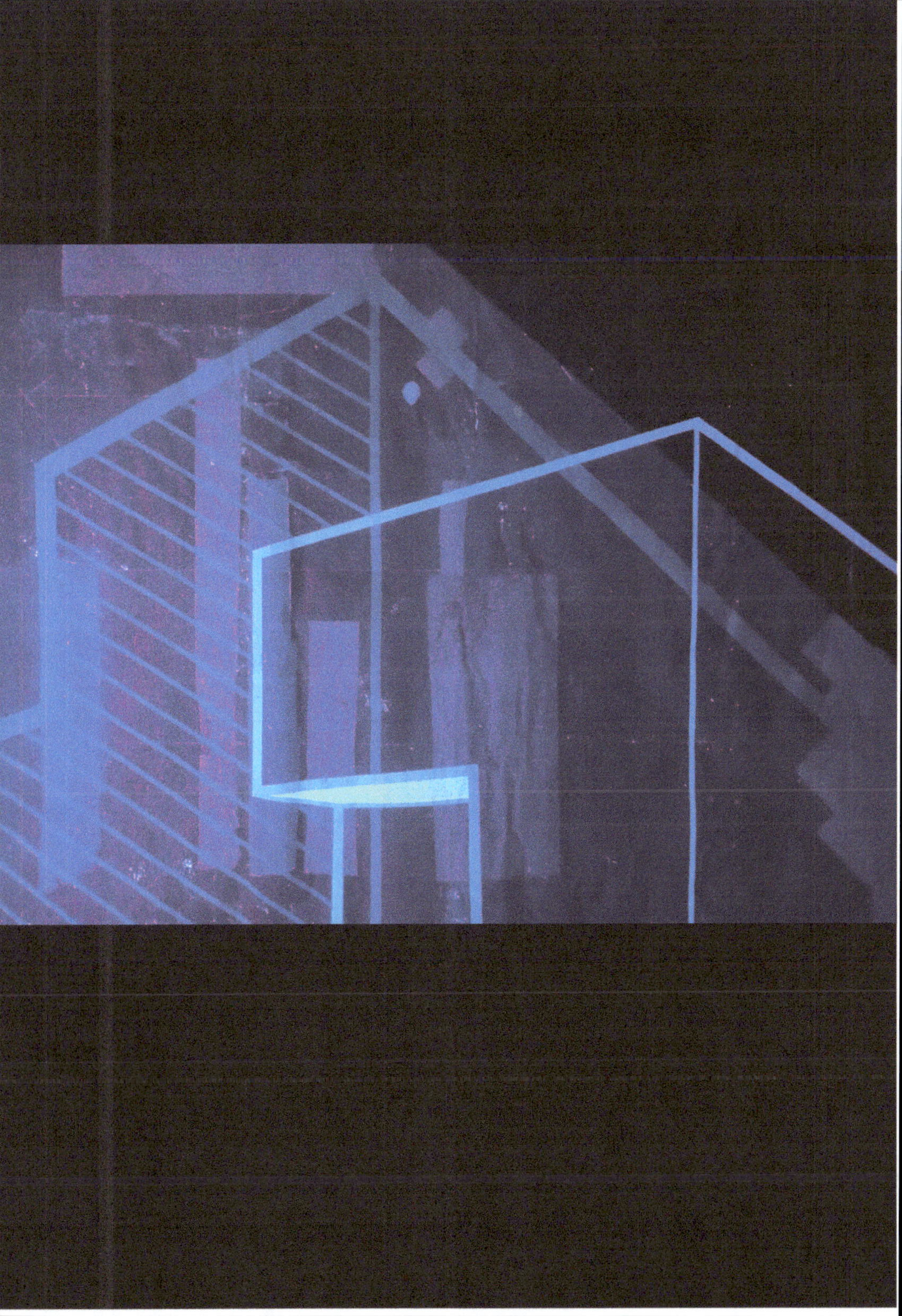

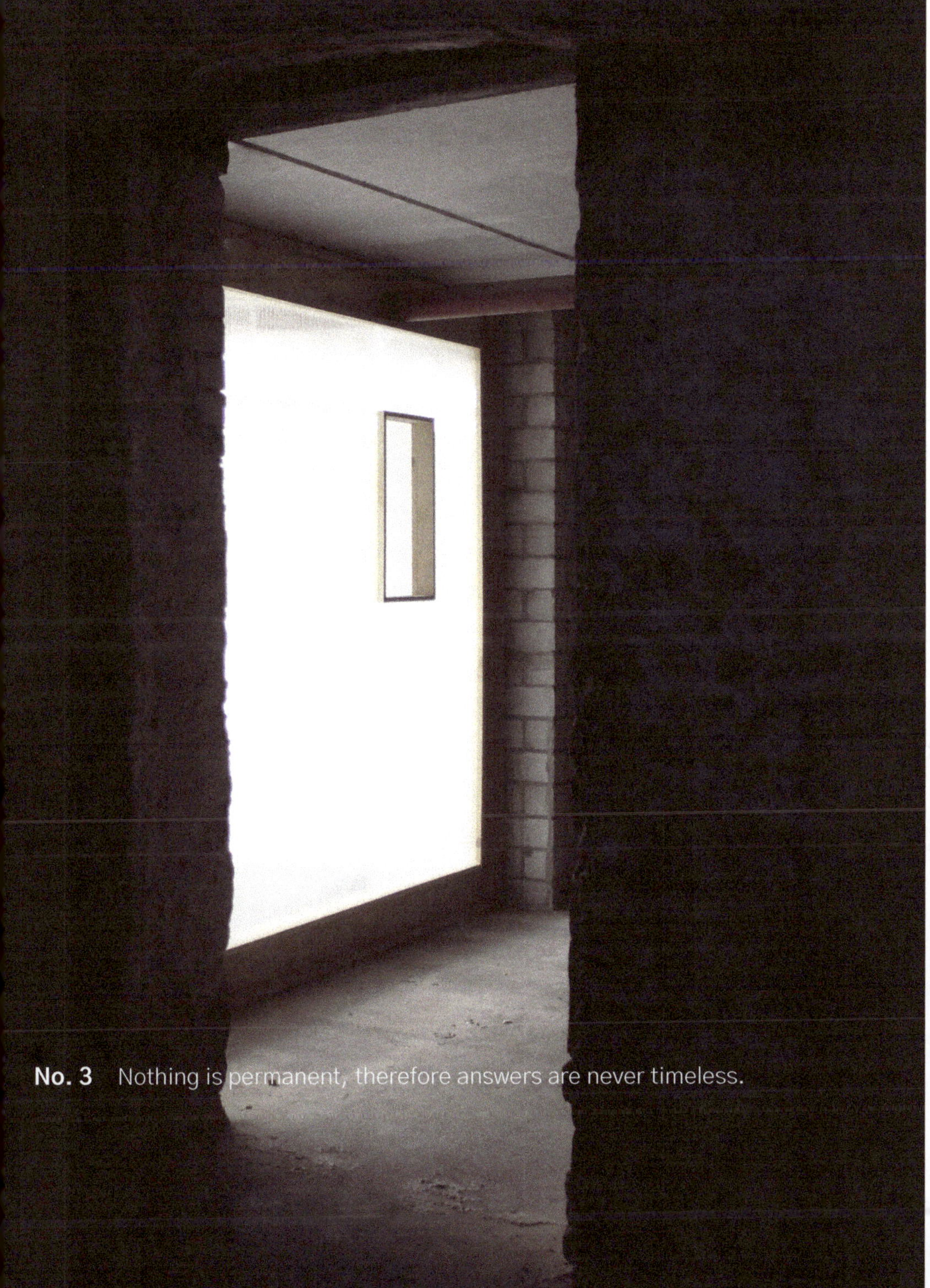

No. 3   Nothing is permanent, therefore answers are never timeless.

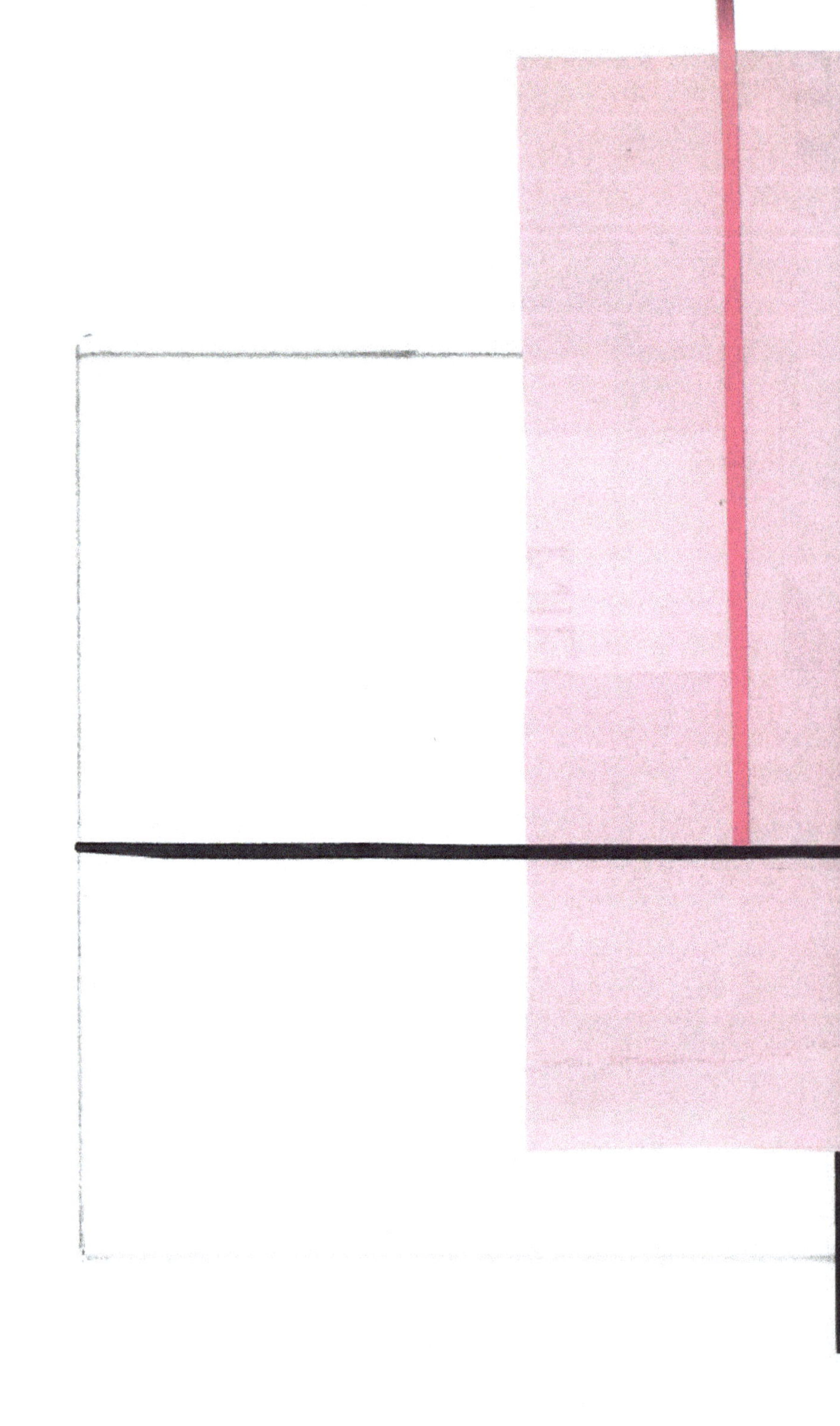

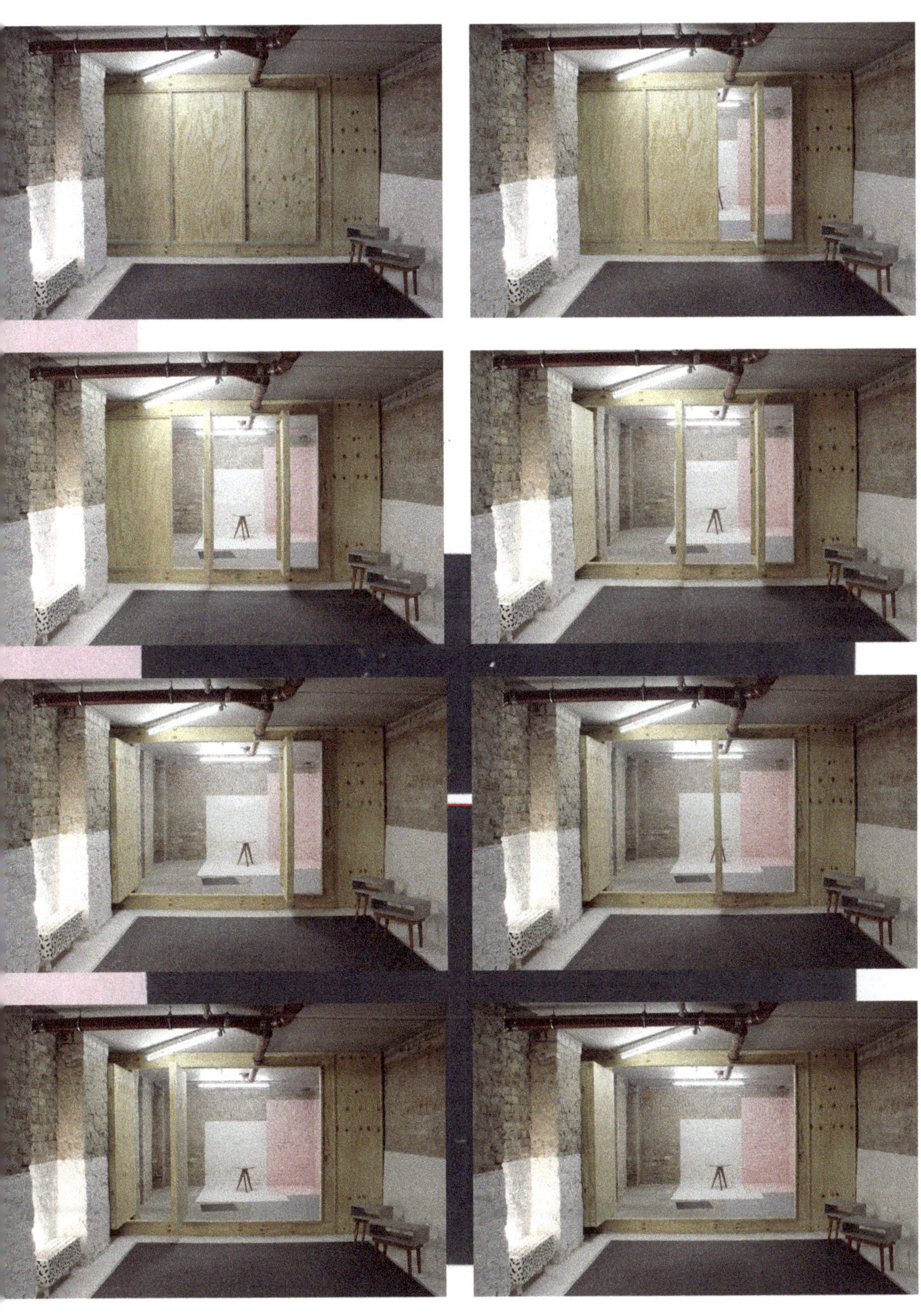

Kardamov Design Studio
So & So Studio

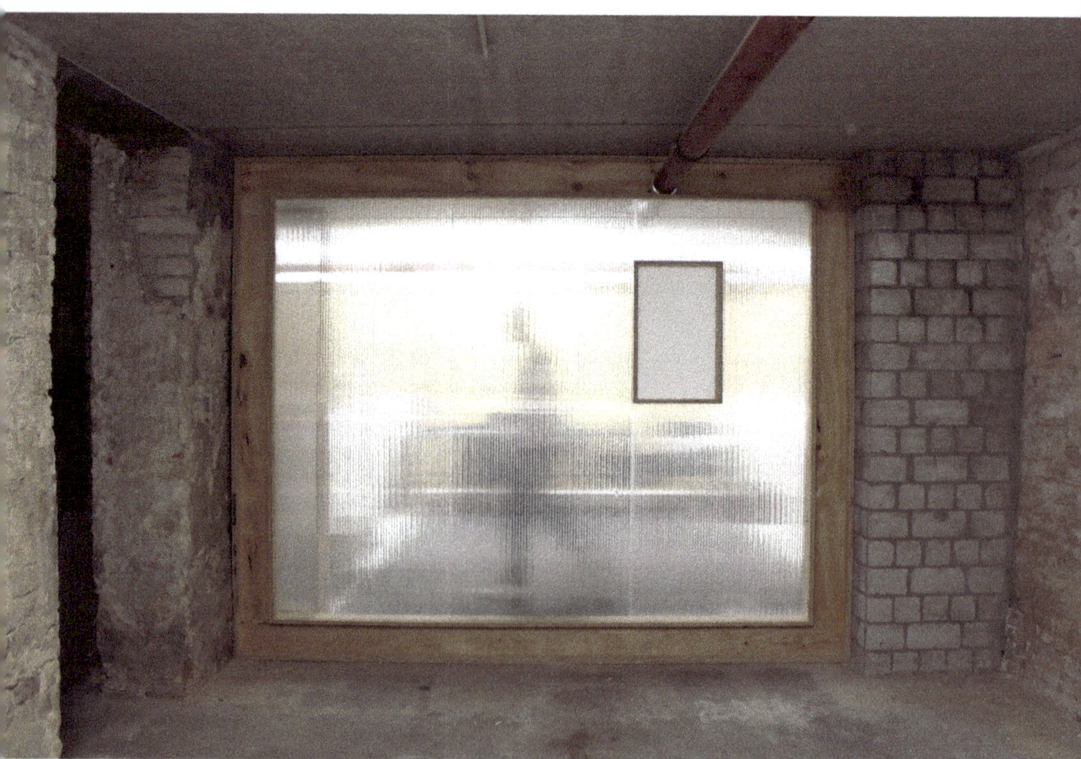

Within the heart of Berlin's creative district, lies a unique working space
for product design and production. Underneath the surface of a courtyard
garden, Kardamov Studio is actively producing and selling concrete furniture
and lighting products between a workshop, design office and product display
space designed by So & So Studio.

The challenge became one of manipulation – a game of creating comfortability
in an otherwise uncomfortable space. Is it possible to create such a space?
– and with such a limited palette, can we then organize the process and aid
in the growth of this designer, as he takes the next step in his career? During
this project we were presented with a number of initial questions. One:
quite simply, how can we create an environment in which our client can sit
comfortably and design his next product? Two: how can we bring natural light,
or the illusion of such light, into a basement space with no windows?

Inspired by the concrete, wood, leather and precious metals of the furniture
being created inside of this working laboratory, So & So Studio faced a lot
of challenges related to subterranean space with clear intent. Due to a lack
of natural daylight and just two existing central heaters to keep workers
motivated through the cold winter, So & So Studio focused their intervention
on emphasizing the rich qualities of raw materials, combined with the blurred
translucency of polycarbonate panels and partial surface treatments.

The resulting intervention defines three very different spaces with flexible
levels of connectivity between them, various techniques of artificial light and a
subtle touch of architectural detailing.

The concrete, wood and metal workshop is a messy space for prototyping,
mixing, cutting and finishing all of the products that come out of Kardamov
Studio. The central office space, linked to the workshop by a small operable
window for small talk, is a room for thinking, drawing, 3D printing of
components and casual client meetings. The third and final space is less
defined; a programmatic blank canvas. Here, Kardamov is able to display,
present and document their final products. The walls between the office
and display space are designed to pivot and slide. As the design process
progresses and the focus shifts, the hierarchy and individuality of the
spaces is allowed to shift and fluctuate too, affording each space the ease
of interaction and the ability to support one another throughout the design
process.

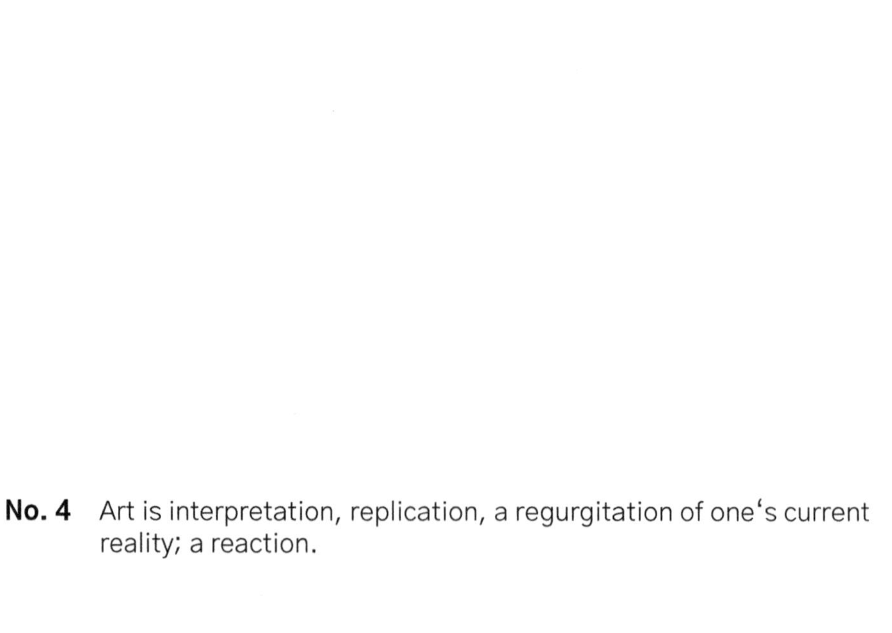

No. 4 Art is interpretation, replication, a regurgitation of one's current reality; a reaction.

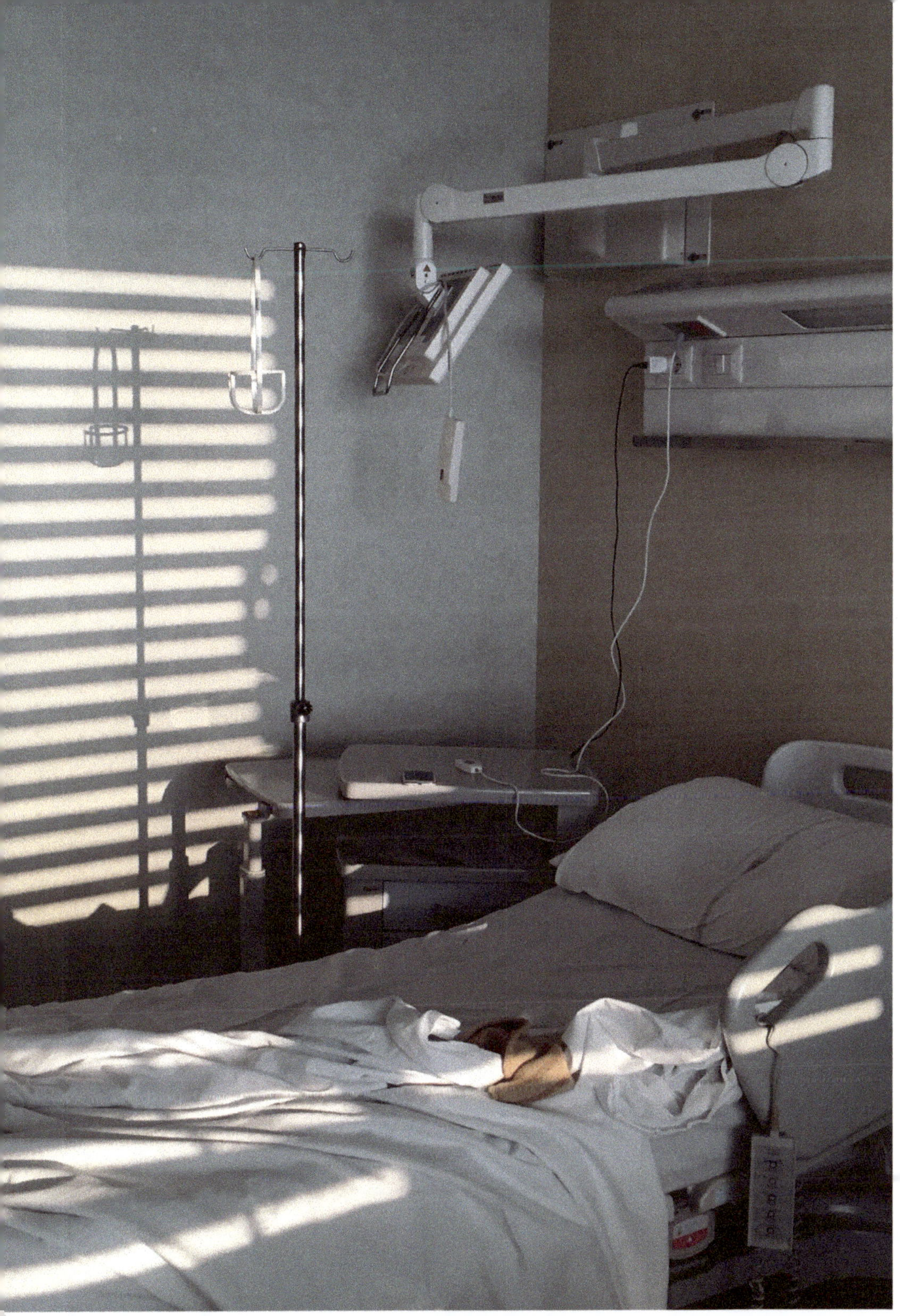

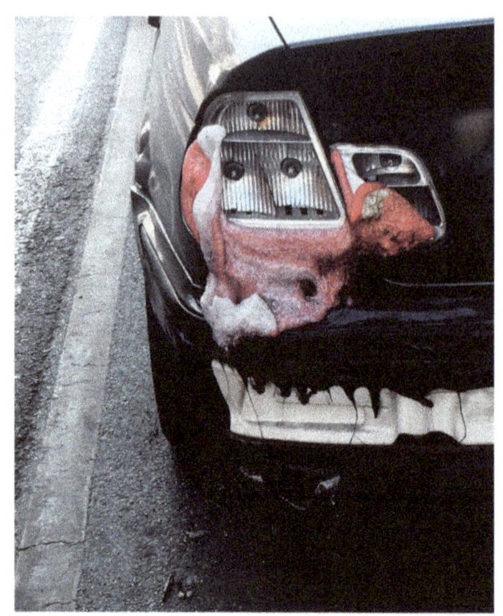
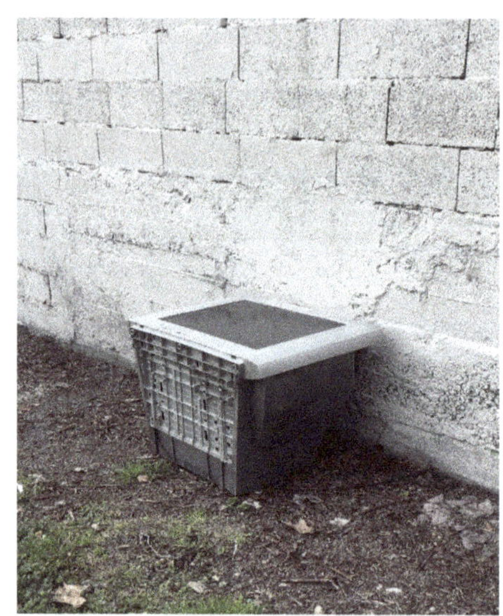
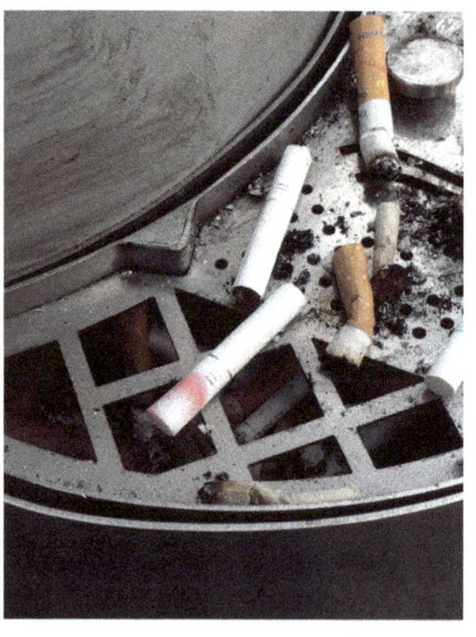
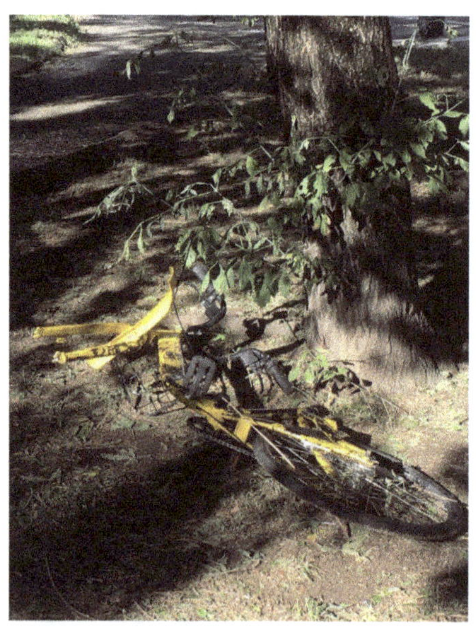

Rejected commodities.
Alessandro Barbieri

Unintended sanctuaries, compositions of discarded wealth, honest representations of an unsustainable economy driven by sincere cynicism.

Corners of humanity filled with micro doses of refused objects extracted from the consumed routine of a neoliberitarian society.

This body of amassed scraps have carved their space in the contemporary scenario becoming essential part of our daily landscape.

A Call for Delusionism
@the.concrete.project

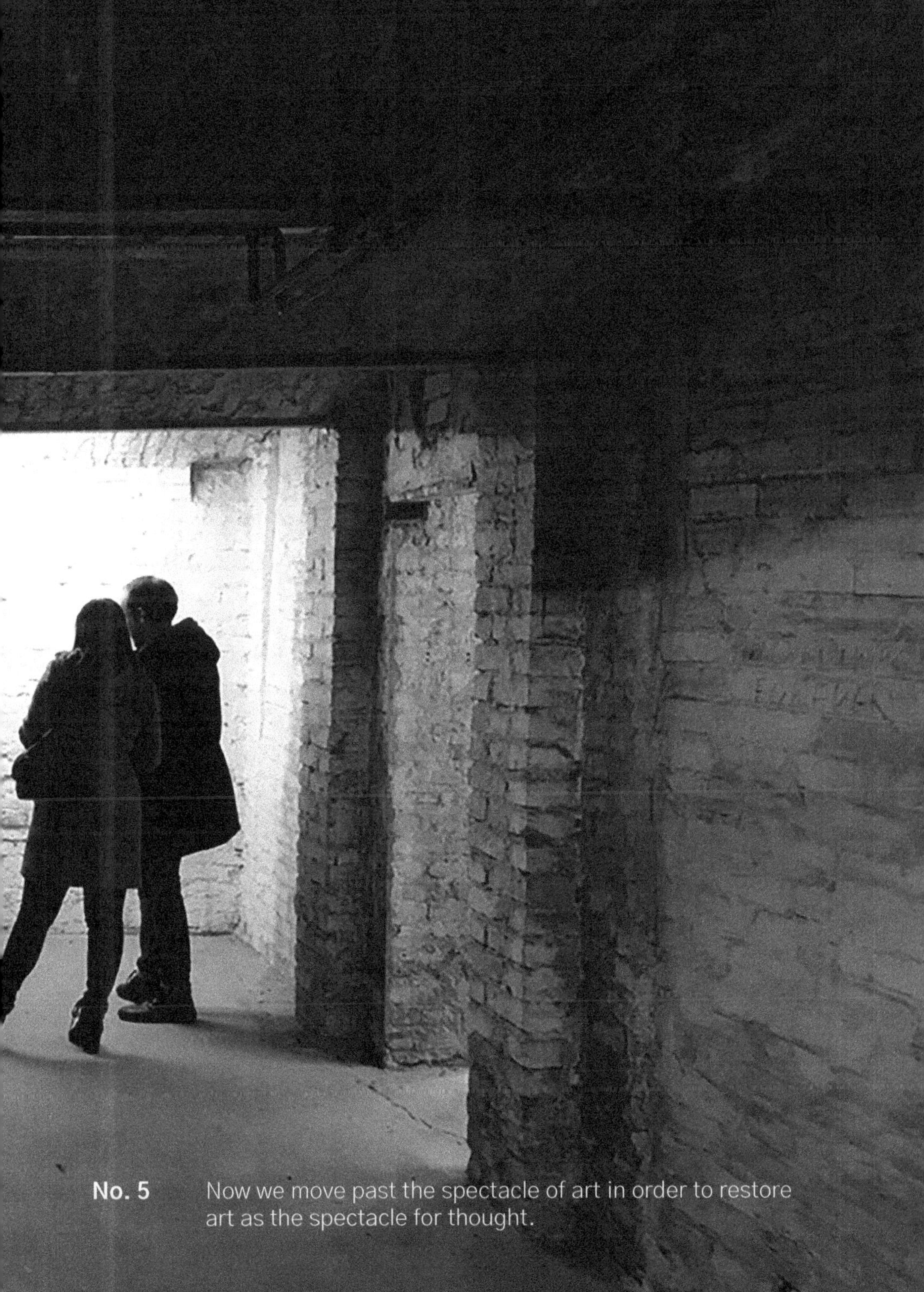

No. 5   Now we move past the spectacle of art in order to restore
art as the spectacle for thought.

A Call for Delusionism

February 01, 2020

Today, we officially announce the beginning of the Delusionist movement.

To be an artist is delusional. Delusionism is but the exploration and progression of the disorientation that we call today's society. In a world where constant disorientation and hysteria has become the norm, truth is the true delusion.

The five points below, offering a minimum definition of Delusionist action, are to be discussed, disputed, fought for, fought against, and continuously tested as a mark of the new decade and a turning point in art history.

No. 1 We trust intuition and human nature before tradition or normality by any means necessary.

No. 2 Intuition is not a feeling. Intuition is the response to a topical understanding of the time.

No. 3 Nothing is permanent, therefore answers are never timeless.

No. 4 Art is interpretation, replication, a regurgitation of one's current reality; a reaction.

No. 5 Now we move past the spectacle of art in order to restore art as the spectacle for thought.

We are Delusionists.

submit

to be considered for **ISM 02**
send submissions to:

we.are.delusionists@gmail.com

soandsostudio.com/delusionism for more info

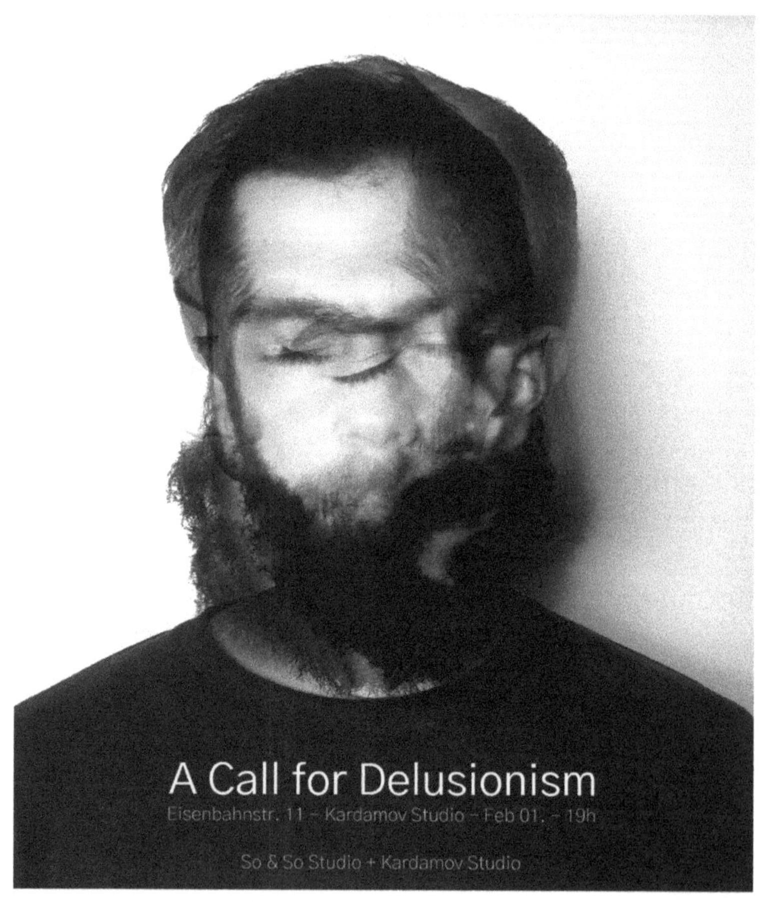

A Call for Delusionism
Eisenbahnstr. 11 – Kardamov Studio – Feb 01. – 19h
So & So Studio + Kardamov Studio

A CALL FOR DELUSION

SATURDAY   01 FEBRUARY 2020 AT 19:00H
SUNDAY   02 FEBRUARY 2020 AT 02:

EISENBAHN STR. 11 BERLIN 10

We're getting ki   out of our studi

we'd like to do two things:

    1.   ve a going away party

    2.   introduce yo   the next step in our delusional thinking
         so join   some drinks and art

doorbell „Kardamov"

…all the way through the two buildings to the back courtyard

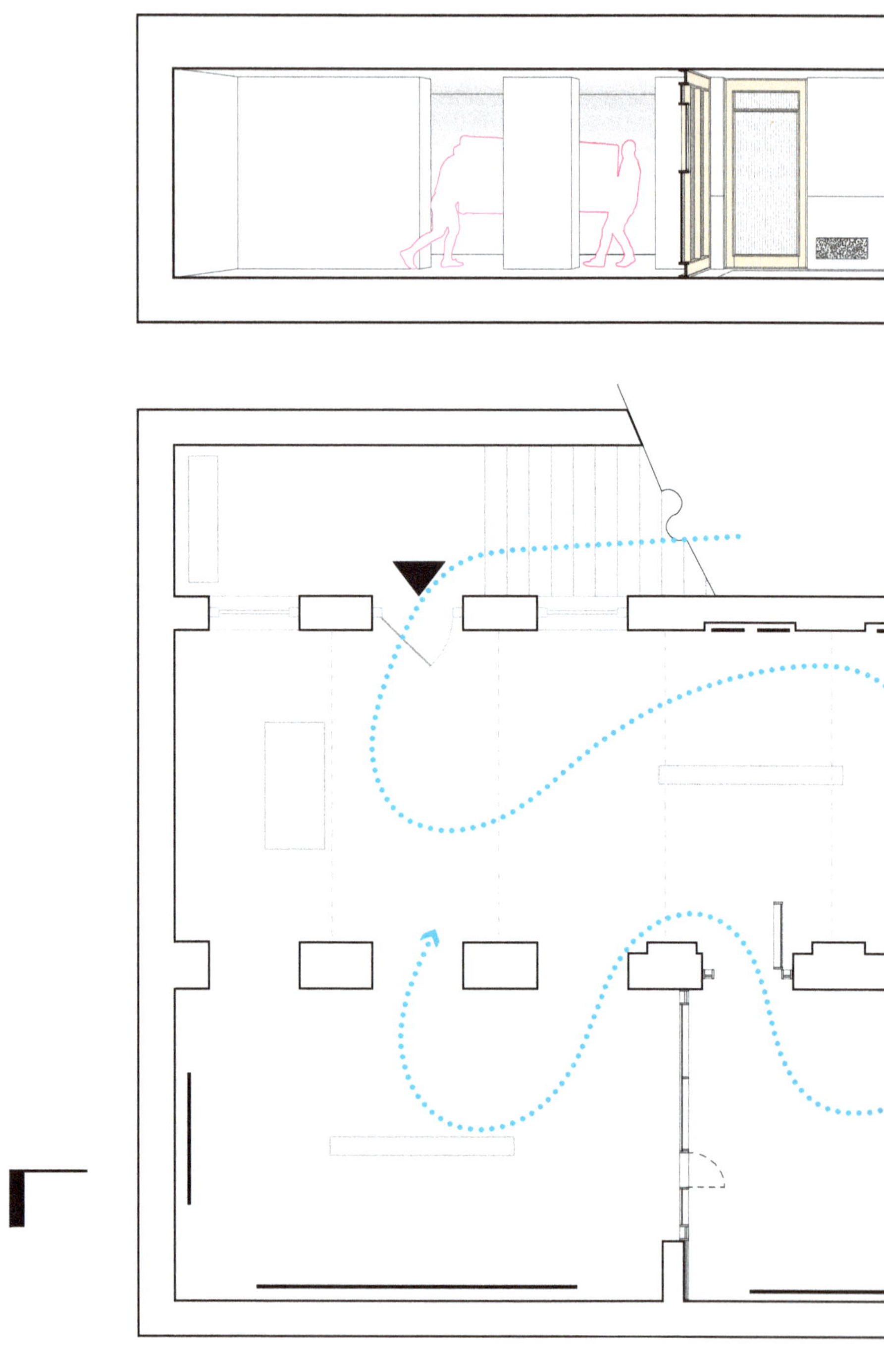

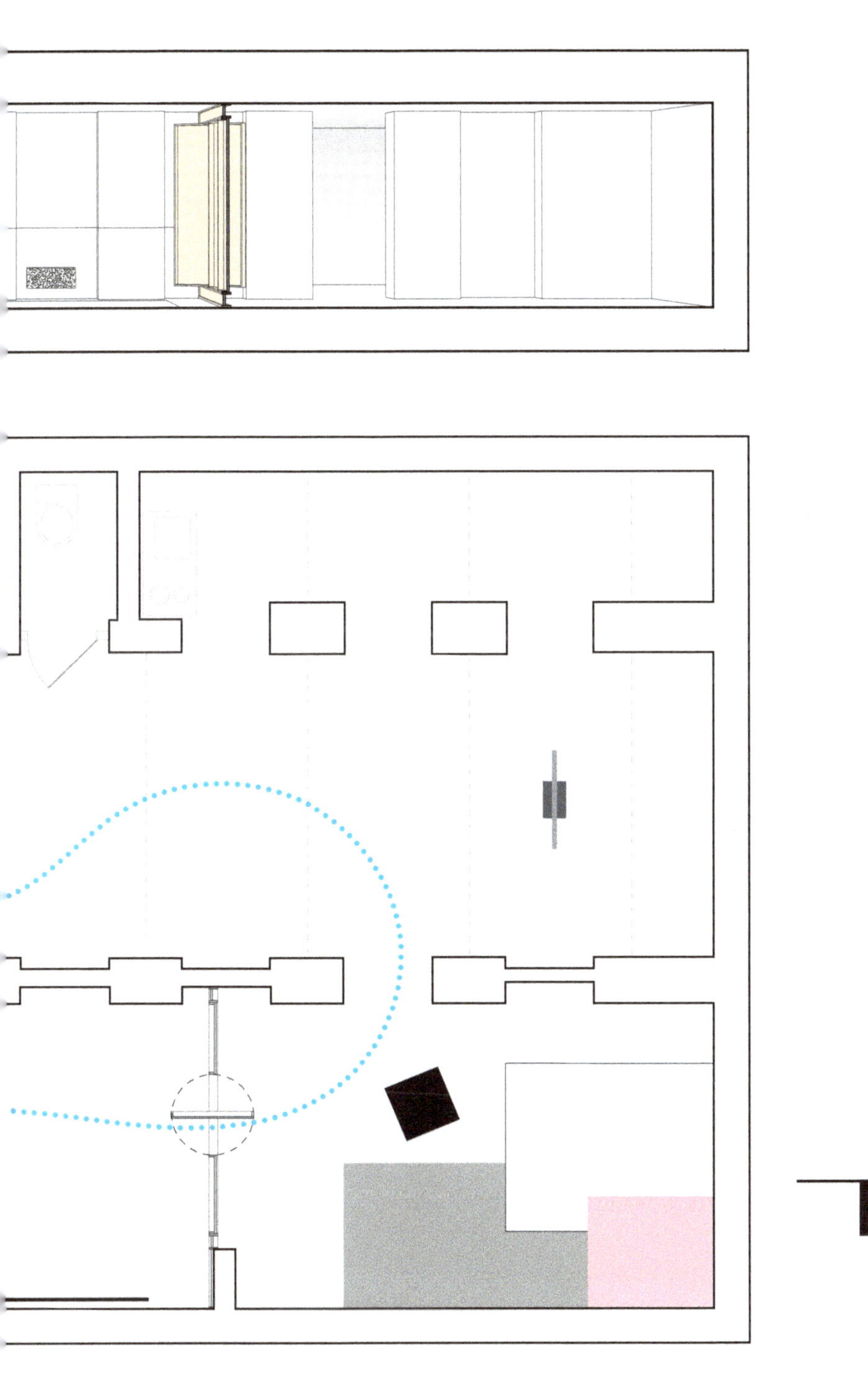

Delusionism
Volume 01

ISBN: 9781716655074 (Paperback)

Front cover image by So & So Studio.
Book design by So & So Studio.

Printed by Lulu Press, Inc.
First printing edition 2020.

www.soandsostudio.com/delusionism

www.ingramcontent.com/pod-product-compliance
Lightning Source LLC
Chambersburg PA
CBHW040807260726
48664CB00030B/1681